KT-117-774

mmm... marshmallows

mmm... marshmallows

Carol Hilker

photography by Steve Painter

LONDON NEW YORK

This book is dedicated to steaming mugs of hot chocolate on cold nights, crisp graham crackers, kindling fires, melted chocolate, cakes that need the perfect frosting, whoopie pies and for those everywhere with a sweet tooth – without you, the marshmallow would be nothing.

Design, photography and prop styling
Steve Painter
Editor Ellen Parnavelas
Production Manager Gordana Simakovic
Art Director Leslie Harrington
Editorial Director Julia Charles

Indexer Hilary Bird
Food styling Lucie McKelvie

First published in 2012 by
Ryland Peters & Small
20–21 Jockey's Fields
London WC1R 4BW
and
519 Broadway, 5th Floor
New York, NY 10012

www.rylandpeters.com

10 9 8 7 6 5 4 3 2 1

Text © Carol Hilker 2012
Design and photographs
© Ryland Peters & Small 2012

Printed in China

ISBN: 978-1-84975-250-3

A CIP record for this book is available from the British Library.

A CIP record for this book is available from the US Library of Congress.

Notes

• All spoon measurements are level unless otherwise specified.

• Ovens should be preheated to the specified temperatures. All ovens work slightly differently. We recommend using an oven thermometer and suggest you consult the maker's handbook for any special instructions, particularly if you are cooking in a fan-assisted/convection oven, as you will need to adjust temperatures according to manufacturer's instructions.

Author's acknowledgements

First and foremost, I want to thank my friends and family for their support, love and constant encouragement. Grandma Stella, this one is for you. I would like to thank Julia Charles and the team at Ryland Peters & Small for making this book happen. From the diligent and patient editing by Ellen Parnavelas; to the wonderful art direction by Leslie Harrington and the beautiful photography and design by Steve Painter. I would also like to thank Anthony Rubinas for his commitment to marshmallow tasting, and, most importantly, for always supporting my creative endeavours, even when they sound like a big pile of fluff (pun intended). Most importantly, this book is ultimately also a product of Misha Wiggins, Michelle Lee and Lori Dooner who taught me everything I know about pastry. Without their mentoring and guidance, I would still be making chocolate sauce in a skillet.

contents

basic vanilla marshmallows

Although many cooks are imtimidated by the idea of marshmallows, in reality they are incredibly simple to make. This recipe is easy to follow and the base for all the others in this book. Once you have mastered it, you will see just how easy it is to prepare endless delicious variations. However you choose to swirl, coat, dust or float your marshmallow, I promise you will enjoy it and become a regular marshmallow maker.

180 g/1½ cups icing/confectioners' sugar, plus an extra 30 g/¼ cup for dusting

60 g/½ cup cornflour/cornstarch

light vegetable oil, for greasing

240 ml/1 cup ice-cold water

3 tablespoons powdered gelatine

400 g/2 cups granulated sugar

120 ml/½ cup golden syrup/light corn syrup

¼ teaspoon fine salt

1 teaspoon vanilla extract

a 33 x 22 x 5-cm/13 x 9 x 2-inch rectangular metal baking pan

Makes about 45 2.5-cm/1-inch cubed marshmallows

Step 1. In a large bowl, sift 180 g/1½ cups of the icing/confectioners' sugar together with the cornflour/cornstarch and set aside.

Step 2. Oil the bottom and sides of the pan, wiping it down with paper towels to remove any excess oil. Dust the bottom and sides of the baking pan liberally with the sifted icing/confectioners' sugar and cornflour/cornstarch mixture.

Step 3. Pour half the water into a large bowl and sprinkle the gelatine over the water. Leave to stand for about 10 minutes.

Step 4. Warm the granulated sugar, golden syrup/light corn syrup, remaining water and salt in a large saucepan set over low heat, stirring continuously with a wooden spoon until the sugar has dissolved. Increase the heat to medium-high and let boil for 10–12 minutes, or until a jam/candy thermometer reaches 116°C/240°F. (This is known as the soft ball stage.) Remove from the heat and pour in the gelatine mixture. Stir with a wooden spoon until the gelatine has dissolved.

Step 5. Use a hand-held mixer to beat the mixture on a high setting for 10 minutes, until thick, shiny and tripled in size.

Step 6. Add the vanilla extract to the marshmallow mixture and mix until just combined, then pour into the greased and sugared pan, working as quickly as possible.

Step 7. Sift the remaining icing/confectioners' sugar evenly over the top and let the marshmallows set at room temperature for at least 4 hours, and up to 1 day until firm.

coat, cut and decorate

To Cut Marshmallows:

When the marshmallows are set in the pan, run a thin butter knife around the edges of the set marshmallows. Turn the pan over onto a cutting board. Lift one corner of the pan and ease the marshmallows out using your fingers. Trim the edges and cut into squares using a large knife, scissors or a pizza cutter coated in oil.

Sift the excess icing/confectioners' sugar and cornflour/cornstarch mixture back into the empty baking pan and roll the individual marshmallows through it to cover. Shake off any excess icing/confectioners' sugar and cornflour/cornstarch before serving or packaging the marshmallows.

Marshmallows can be stored at room temperature for up to a week. However, if you have a warm kitchen, refrigerating the marshmallows is recommended.

For Mini Marshmallows:

Use a piping bag to make pretty mini marshmallows. After preparing the marshmallow mixture in your chosen flavour, immediately put the mixture in a piping bag and pipe out your mini marshmallows. Leave to set.

To Cover In Chocolate:

Line a baking sheet with parchment paper. Put the chocolate in a heatproof bowl set over a pan of gently simmering water. Stir until the chocolate melts and is smooth. (Milk chocolate and white chocolate melt quickly and will burn if not watched and stirred often.) Remove from heat and let cool.

Once the chocolate has cooled to room temperature, work quickly, dipping each marshmallow in the melted chocolate using a fork, to cover each marshmallow.

vegan marshmallows

There is no need to use animal products to make the perfect marshmallow. You can use guar gum, soya/soy protein isolate and a vegetarian gelatine to create delicious vegan marshmallows and marshmallow treats. To make different flavours, simply replace the water in the recipe with your choice of fruit juice.

180 g/1½ cups icing/
confectioners' sugar, plus an
extra 30 g/¼ cup for dusting

60 g/½ cup cornflour/cornstarch

light vegetable oil, for greasing

5 tablespoons soya/soy protein
isolate 90%

2 teaspoons baking powder

¼ teaspoon guar gum

310 ml/1¼ cups cold water

1 tablespoon Vege Gel, Genutine
Vegetarian Gelatine or similar

310 g/1½ cups unrefined/raw
sugar

340 g/1 cup golden syrup/light
corn syrup

2 teaspoons vanilla extract

Makes 30–35 2.5-cm/1-inch cubed
marshmallows

In a large bowl, sift 180 g/1½ cups of the icing/confectioners' sugar together with the cornflour/cornstarch and set aside.

Oil the bottom and sides of the baking pan, wiping down the pan with paper towels to remove any excess oil. Sift the bottom and sides of the baking pan liberally with the icing/confectioners' sugar and cornflour/cornstarch mixture.

Mix the soya/soy protein, baking powder and guar gum together in a stand mixer. Add 180 ml/¾ cup cold water and beat on high for 10 minutes until stiff peaks form. Set aside.

Mix the gelatine and unrefined/raw sugar in a large saucepan. Add the remaining water and whisk quickly until thick. Stir in the golden syrup/light corn syrup. Set the saucepan on the stovetop over low heat. Cook the mixture until it reaches 110°C/230°F on a jam/candy thermometer, stirring occasionally. Remove the pan from the heat and quickly stir in the vanilla extract.

Slowly add the hot syrup to the soya/soy protein mixture with the stand mixer set on high as you pour in the syrup. Beat the mixture on high for 10 minutes.

Pour the mixture into the greased and sugared pan, working as quickly as possible. Sift the remaining icing/confectioners' sugar evenly over the top and let the marshmallows set in the refrigerator for at least 1 hour until firm.

marshmallow fluff

Marshmallow fluff is a great way to add the taste of melted marshmallows to sandwiches, cake fillings or ice cream toppings. Making fluff is different from making marshmallows because the corn syrup is cooked to a higher temperature, using no gelatine.

In the bowl of a stand mixer fitted with a whisk attachment, beat the egg whites until light and frothy. Slowly pour in 2 tablespoons of sugar, leaving the mixer running. Beat the mixture until stiff peaks form and set aside.

Put the water, the golden syrup/light corn syrup and the remaining sugar in a small saucepan and stir to combine. Set the saucepan on the stovetop over medium heat and bring to the boil. Cook for about 6 minutes, or until the mixture reaches 127°C/260°F on a jam/candy thermometer, then remove from the heat.

Slowly add the hot syrup to the egg white mixture, with the stand mixer set on low as you pour in the syrup. Increase the speed to high and continue to beat for 5 minutes. Add the vanilla extract and beat for no more than 1 minute until the mixture starts to resemble marshmallow fluff.

Pour the fluff into a lidded plastic container or a large screwtop jar. The fluff should be stored in the refrigerator where it will keep for up to 1 week.

3 large egg whites, at room temperature

150 g/¾ cup plus 2 tablespoons granulated sugar

100 ml/⅓ cup water

255 g/¾ cup golden syrup/ light corn syrup

2 teaspoons vanilla extract

Makes about 500 g/5 cups

simple

cinnamon marshmallows

Subtly spiced with cinnamon and vanilla, these warming marshmallows will surprise you with their rich flavour. They are best enjoyed on a cold winter's day, floated on top of a steaming mug of milky hot chocolate.

Basic Vanilla Marshmallows (see page 6 but follow method here)

1½ tablespoons ground cinnamon

3 cinnamon sticks, lightly crushed in a tea ball

To serve

hot chocolate

cocoa powder, for dusting

a small, round cookie cutter (optional)

Makes about 45 x 2.5-cm/1-inch round or cubed marshmallows

Prepare the marshmallows according to the recipe for Basic Vanilla Marshmallows on page 6, adding the ground cinnamon to the icing/confectioners' sugar mixture in Step 1.

In Step 4, add the tea ball filled with crushed cinnamon sticks to the saucepan with the sugar, golden syrup/light corn syrup, water and salt. When all the sugar has dissolved, remove from the heat and let the cinnamon steep into the mixture for about 30 minutes, before removing the tea ball. Return the saucepan to the heat and complete Step 4.

Complete Steps 5–7 and when the marshmallows are set, stamp out small rounds with the cookie cutter. Serve the marshmallows floating on mugs of hot cocoa and lightly dusted with cocoa powder.

toasted coconut marshmallows

Toasted coconut marshmallows are an all-time classic confection. Here the marshmallow is flavoured with coconut extract and topped with scrumptious toasted coconut. Perfect for a tropical tea time treat!

90 g/4 cups dessicated coconut

Basic Vanilla Marshmallows (see page 6 but follow method here) excluding the icing/confectioners' sugar, cornflour/cornstarch and oil

1 teaspoon coconut extract

Makes about 45 x 2.5-cm/1-inch cubed marshmallows

To toast the coconut, preheat the oven to 160°C/325°F/Gas 2. Lay the dessicated coconut out on a baking sheet and bake for 7 minutes, stirring half-way through. Turn the oven off and let the coconut bake in the cooling oven for 15 minutes, stirring occasionally. Remove from the oven and set aside.

Follow the recipe for Basic Vanilla Marshmallows on page 6, omitting steps 1 and 2. Cover the bottom and sides of the baking pan with half the toasted coconut, covering the bottom completely with a thick layer.

Prepare the marshmallows according to Steps 3–7 of the recipe for Basic Vanilla Marshmallows on page 6, adding the coconut extract with the vanilla extract in Step 6.

Sift the rest of the toasted coconut evenly over the top before completing Step 7 and leaving the marshmallows to set. Cut into cubes to serve.

chocolate marshmallows

There is nothing more heavenly than a luxurious, chocolate treat. These rich chocolate-rippled marshmallows will delight any chocolate-lover. You could even coat them with melted chocolate to enjoy the ultimate in chocolate indulgence. Serve with warming cups of black coffee, or better still package and give as a gift to your favourite chocaholic!

50 g/½ cup plus 2 tablespoons cocoa powder

4 tablespoons boiling water

Basic Vanilla Marshmallows (see page 6 but follow method here)

Makes about 45 x 2.5-cm/1-inch cubed marshmallows

Stir the 50 g/½ cup of cocoa powder with the boiling water in a small bowl and whisk thoroughly to dissolve the cocoa. Set aside.

Prepare the marshmallows according to the recipe for Basic Vanilla Marshmallows on page 6, adding 2 tablespoons of cocoa powder to the the icing/confectioners' sugar mixture in Step 1.

After completing Step 5, pour the cocoa mixture into the middle of the marshmallow and stir with a wooden spoon, until the cocoa powder is swirled throughout.

Complete Steps 6 and 7 and coat with melted chocolate (see page 7), if desired.

peppermint marshmallows

Peppermint marshmallows are a refreshing yet sweet treat and delicious with a cup of hot chocolate. Top them with a sprinkle of crushed candy canes and present them in a box for a cute festive gift.

Basic Vanilla Marshmallows (see page 6 but follow method here)

2 teaspoons peppermint extract

red food colouring (optional)

crushed candy canes, to decorate

Makes about 45 x 2.5-cm/1-inch cubed marshmallows

Prepare the marshmallows according to the recipe for Basic Vanilla Marshmallows on page 6, adding the peppermint extract with the vanilla extract in Step 6.

Add 4 or 5 drops of red food colouring to the mixture (if using), before spreading the mixture in the pan. Using a spatula, mix in the red food colouring to create a swirl taking care not to stir the food colouring in completely. Pour the swirled mixture into the prepared pan and spread evenly.

Complete Step 7 and when the marshmallows are set, top with crushed candy canes to decorate.

peanut butter and jelly marshmallows

Peanut butter and jelly is one of the most famous flavour combinations. These marshmallows use grape jelly instead of syrup to infuse the flavour. Sandwich the marshmallows between peanut butter cookies to create a sweet variation of your favourite lunchtime snack – perfect for serving with morning coffee or afternoon tea with friends.

Basic Vanilla Marshmallows (see page 6 but follow method here)

245 g/¾ cup grape jelly (to replace the golden syrup/light corn syrup)

store-bought or home-baked peanut butter cookies, to serve

Makes about 45 x 2.5-cm/1-inch cubed marshmallows

Prepare the marshmallows according to the recipe for Basic Vanilla Marshmallows on page 6, replacing the golden syrup/ light corn syrup with grape jelly in Step 4.

Preheat the oven to 150°C (300°F) Gas 2.

To assemble, sandwich your finished marshmallows between two peanut butter cookies and warm in the preheated oven for a minute or so to melt the marshmallows. Serve warm.

banana and peanut butter swirled marshmallows

Melted peanut butter is swirled through these decadent marshmallows to give the smooth, nutty contrast to the fresh taste of banana.

280 g/10 oz smooth peanut butter

Basic Vanilla Marshmallows (see page 6 but follow method here)

250 ml/1 cup cold banana juice/nectar

Makes 45 x 2.5-cm/1-inch cubed marshmallows

Put the peanut butter in a small saucepan set on the stovetop over low heat. Heat the peanut butter until it melts to a smooth, pouring consistency.

Prepare the marshmallows according to the recipe for Basic Vanilla Marshmallows on page 6, replacing the water with banana juice/nectar in Steps 3 and 4.

After mixing in the vanilla extract in Step 6, pour the melted peanut butter into the middle of the mixture. Using a wooden spoon, mix in the melted peanut butter to create a swirl taking care not to stir it in completely. Pour the swirled marshmallow mixture into the prepared pan and spread evenly.

Complete Step 7 and when the marshmallows are set, serve as they are or coat with melted chocolate, if desired. (see page 7).

swirls

chocolate-covered caramel swirl marshmallows

Reminiscent of chocolate-covered marshmallow and caramel truffles, this indulgent recipe brings you the best of both worlds. The marshmallow is a classic vanilla confection swirled with caramel sauce and finished with a glossy coating of melted dark chocolate.

Basic Vanilla Marshmallows (see page 6 but follow method here)

225 g/8 oz store-bought caramel sauce

250 g/1⅔ cup dark chocolate chips, melted

Makes 45 x 2.5-cm/1-inch cubed marshmallows

Prepare the marshmallows according to the recipe for Basic Vanilla Marshmallows on page 6. After mixing in the vanilla extract in Step 6, pour the caramel sauce into the middle of the mixture. Using a wooden spoon, mix in the caramel to create a swirl taking care not stir the caramel in completely. Pour the swirled marshmallow mixture into the prepared pan and spread evenly.

Complete Step 7 and when the marshmallows are set, cut and coat with the melted chocolate chips according to the instructions on page 7.

champagne and strawberry swirl marshmallows

This is one of my most luxurious recipes. The elegant flavours of champagne and strawberry work well together to make a sophisticated mouthful.

Basic Vanilla Marshmallows (see page 6 but follow method here)

300 g/2 cups fresh strawberries

125 ml/1 cup cold, flat champagne

a small heart-shaped cookie cutter (optional)

Makes 45 x small heart-shaped or 2.5-cm/1-inch cubed marshmallows

To make the strawberry purée, hull the strawberries and cut them into 2.5-cm/1-inch pieces. Put them in a small saucepan set on the stovetop over low heat and cook for 5 minutes. Remove from the heat and let cool. When cool, transfer to a food processor and process until puréed. Strain the purée through a sieve/strainer. You should have 250 ml/1 cup of purée.

Prepare the marshmallows according to the recipe for Basic Vanilla Marshmallows on page 6, replacing the water with the champagne in Steps 3 and 4

After mixing in the vanilla extract in Step 6, pour the strawberry purée into the middle of the mixture. Using a wooden spoon, mix in the purée to create a swirl taking care not to stir it in completely. Pour the swirled marshmallow mixture into the prepared pan and spread evenly.

Complete Step 7 and when the marshmallows are set, stamp out hearts with the cookie cutter before serving.

apple-caramel swirl marshmallows

An apple-caramel swirl marshmallow is the perfect autumnal treat to accompany a cup of hot, spiced cider or tea. These delicious seasonal treats are perfect served at a halloween gathering for friends and family.

Basic Vanilla Marshmallows (see page 6 but follow method here)

225 g/8 oz store-bought caramel or toffee sauce

250 ml/1 cup cold apple juice/nectar

1 tablespoon Calvados (optional)

Makes 45 x 2.5-cm/1-inch cubed marshmallows

Prepare the marshmallows according to the recipe for Basic Vanilla Marshmallows on page 6, replacing the water with cold apple juice/nectar* in Steps 3 and 4.

Mix in the calvados (if using) with the vanilla extract in Step 6, then pour the caramel sauce into the middle of the mixture. Using a wooden spoon, stir in the caramel sauce to create a swirl, taking care not mix it in completely. Pour the swirled marshmallow mixture into the prepared pan and spread evenly.

Complete Step 7 and when the marshmallows are set, cut into slices or cubes and serve with a cup of hot, spiced cider or tea.

*To enhance the delicious taste of apples, try to find canned apple nectar instead of apple juice as the flavour is much more intense.

merlot and chocolate
swirled marshmallows

The smokiness of a good red wine mixed with dark chocolate is a perfect flavour combination. This marshmallow is a delicious pairing of the two, creating an elegant marshmallow treat for sophisticated tastebuds.

Basic Vanilla Marshmallows (see page 6 but follow method here)

250 ml/1 cup cold merlot (or other full-bodied red wine)

For the chocolate sauce:

150 g/1 cup dark chocolate chips

30 g/2 tablespoons butter

30 ml/2 tablespoons cold water

400-g/14-oz can sweetened condensed milk

1 teaspoon vanilla extract

Makes 45 x 2.5-cm/1-inch cubed marshmallows.

To prepare the chocolate sauce, put all the ingredients in a small saucepan set on the stovetop. Gently melt, stirring continuously, until smooth. Remove from the heat and stir in the vanilla extract. Set aside and leave to cool.

Prepare the marshmallows according to the recipe for Basic Vanilla Marshmallows on page 6, replacing the water with the merlot in Steps 3 and 4.

Omit the vanilla extract in Step 6 and pour the cooled chocolate sauce into the middle of the mixture. Using a wooden spoon, stir in the chocolate sauce to create a swirl taking care not mix it in completely. Pour the mixture into the prepared pan and spread evenly.

Complete Step 7 and when the marshmallows are set, cut and serve as they are or coat with the melted chocolate chips according to the instructions on page 7.

beverage

cafe mocha marshmallows

These delicious treats have the rich, deep flavour of a cup of coffee with cream and sugar. Serve them floating on top of a hot cup of black coffee dusted with cocoa powder for a chocolate mocha treat. They also make a great addition to a cappuccino or latte instead of whipped cream.

Basic Vanilla Marshmallows (see page 6 but follow method here)

1 tablespoon instant ground coffee

cocoa powder, to serve

Makes about 45 x 2.5-cm/1-inch cubed marshmallows

Prepare the marshmallows according to the recipe for Basic Vanilla Marshmallows on page 6, adding the instant ground coffee to the water and gelatine in Step 3.

Complete Step 7 and when the marshmallows are set, cut and serve floating on top of hot cups of black coffee, dusted with cocoa powder. (Alternatively, dust with ground cinnamon or cinnamon sugar to add a touch of spice.)

milk chocolate-covered stout marshmallows with pretzels

From cakes to marshmallows, stout mixed with chocolate always leads to a winning flavour. These eyecatching marshmallows are flavoured with stout, smothered in milk chocolate and topped with white chocolate-covered pretzels for added crunch.

Basic Vanilla Marshmallows (see page 6 but follow method here)

250 ml/1 cup cold, flat stout (such as Guinness)

350 g/14 oz milk or dark chocolate chips

store-bought white or milk chocolate-covered pretzels

Makes 45 x 2.5-cm/1-inch cubed marshmallows

Prepare the marshmallows according to the recipe for Basic Vanilla Marshmallows on page 6, replacing the water with the stout in Steps 3 and 4.

Complete Step 7 and when the marshmallows are set, cut and coat with the melted chocolate chips according to the instructions on page 7.

Top each coated marshmallow with a chocolate-covered pretzel for the perfect finish.

earl grey and orange marshmallows

These elegant marshmallows have the subtle aroma and taste of bergamot that you find in a cup of Earl Grey tea. A refreshing hint of citrus is provided by the orange zest, making them a delicious and unusual tea time treat.

Basic Vanilla Marshmallows (see page 6 but follow method here)

250 ml/1 cup cold, strong earl grey tea

1 tablespoon finely grated orange zest (from an unwaxed fruit)

Makes about 45 x 2.5-cm/1-inch cubed marshmallows

Prepare the marshmallows according to the recipe for Basic Vanilla Marshmallows on page 6, replacing the water with the tea in Steps 3 and 4, and the vanilla extract with grated orange zest in Step 6.

Complete Step 7 and when the marshmallows are set, cut into cubes and serve each cube on a teaspoon as a perfect bite-size treat.

rootbeer float marshmallows

These fun, retro treats have all the authentic tastes of a classic soda fountain ice cream float. For an extra special treat, serve them topped with a swirl of whipped cream and a sprinkling of crushed ice cream wafers.

Basic Vanilla Marshmallows (see page 6 but follow method here)

2 litres/2 quarts rootbeer (or 1 litre/1 quart rootbeer plus 1 litre/1 quart cream soda, orange soda or grape soda)

whipped cream and crushed ice cream wafers, to serve

Makes about 45 x 2.5-cm/1-inch cubed marshmallows

To make the syrup, pour the rootbeer into a large saucepan set on the stovetop over high heat and bring to the boil. Lower the heat to medium-high and cook until the liquid reduces to 375 ml/1½ cups. Let cool slightly.

Prepare the marshmallows according to the recipe for Basic Vanilla Marshmallows on page 6, adding the soda syrup to the mixture in Step 4.

Complete Step 7 and when the marshmallows are set, serve topped with whipped cream and crushed wafers.

Irish cream marshmallows

These light-as-air, creamy marshmallows are for adults only and turn an ordinary cup of black coffee into a decadent Irish coffee – the perfect after dinner indulgence.

Basic Vanilla Marshmallows (see page 6 but follow method here)

2 tablespoons Irish cream liqueur (such as Baileys)

freshly-brewed black coffee, to serve

heatproof glasses and spoons

Makes about 45 x 2.5-cm/1-inch cubed marshmallows

Prepare the marshmallows according to the recipe for Basic Vanilla Marshmallows on page 6, adding the Irish cream liqueur with the vanilla extract in Step 6.

Complete Step 7 and when the marshmallows are set, cut into cubes.

Serve floating on top of a glass of hot coffee with a spoon on the side, for an extra-luxurious treat.

strawberry malted marshmallows

Strawberry malts are an old-time soda fountain favourite. This marshmallow takes a strawberry marshmallow and mixes it with malt powder to create a tasty and colourful nod to summer. (You will need malt powder, not sweetened malted milk.)

250 ml/1 cup cold, strawberry purée (see page 25)

2 tablespoons malt powder

Basic Vanilla Marshmallows (see page 6 but follow method here)

finely ground, freeze-dried strawberries mixed with a little cornflour/cornstarch

Makes about 45 x 2.5-cm/1-inch cubed marshmallows

Mix the strawberry purée with the malt powder and set the mixture aside.

Prepare the marshmallows according to the recipe for Basic Vanilla Marshmallows on page 6, reducing the quantity of cold water to 180ml/¾ cup and adding the strawberry purée and malt mixture to the water and gelatine in Step 3.

Complete Step 7 and when the marshmallows are set, serve as they are or coat with the freeze-dried strawberry mixture, if desired.

fruity

meyer lemon marshmallows

The Meyer lemon has a distinct flavour. Unlike a traditional lemon, which is tart and sour, the Meyer lemon is slightly sweeter due to a cross-pollination with a mandarin. During the winter months, when the Meyer lemon is in season, these marshmallows are wonderful served with hot lemon tea or earl grey.

Basic Vanilla Marshmallows (see page 6 but follow method here)

250 ml/1 cup ice cold Meyer lemon juice

1 tablespoon finely grated Meyer lemon zest (from an unwaxed fruit)

Makes about 45 x 2.5-cm/1-inch cubed marshmallows

Prepare the marshmallows according to the recipe for Basic Vanilla Marshmallows on page 6, replacing the water with lemon juice in Steps 3 and 4 and omitting the vanilla extract.

Complete Step 7 and when the marshmallows are set, serve as they are or to accompany a cup of hot lemon tea or earl grey.

Orange, lime or grapefruit juice can also be used here as alternatives to Meyer lemon.

spiced cranberry marshmallows

These warming marshmallows are reminiscent of traditional holiday cranberry sauce. Mixing the cranberry with orange zest and a variety of spices makes them the perfect treat to enjoy with green tea or mulled apple cider.

½ teaspoon ground ginger

½ teaspoon ground nutmeg

250 ml/1 cup cold cranberry juice concentrate

Basic Vanilla Marshmallows (see page 6 but follow method here)

1 teaspoon finely grated orange zest (from an unwaxed fruit)

Makes about 45 x 2.5-cm/1-inch cubed marshmallows

Mix the ground ginger and nutmeg with the cold cranberry juice concentrate.

Prepare the marshmallows according to the recipe for Basic Vanilla Marshmallows on page 6, replacing the water with the cranberry juice mixture in Steps 3 and 4, and the vanilla extract with orange zest in Step 6.

Complete Step 7 and when the marshmallows are set, cut into cubes to serve.

raspberry and rosewater marshmallows

Raspberry marshmallows are such a treat. They are even more perfect when dipped in luxurious dark chocolate. Add a little rosewater and you have a perfumed, yet sweet marshmallow that is a little more sophisticated than your average confection.

125 g/1 cup frozen or fresh raspberries

Basic Vanilla Marshmallows (see page 6 but follow method here)

1 teaspoon of rosewater (optional)

250 g/1⅓ cup dark chocolate chips

Makes about 45 x 2.5-cm/1-inch cubed marshmallows

To prepare the raspberry purée, put the raspberries in a small saucepan set on the stovetop and gently heat until softened, mashing with a spoon to create a purée. Continue to heat gently until the mixture has reduced to about 100 ml/⅓ cup then strain through a sieve/strainer to remove the seeds and set the raspberry purée aside.

Prepare the marshmallows according to the recipe for Basic Vanilla Marshmallows on page 6, adding the raspberry purée in Step 4 after pouring in the gelatine mixture.

Complete Step 7 and when the marshmallows are set, cut and coat with the melted chocolate chips according to the instructions on page 7.

These make an elegant gift so try presenting them as you would luxury chocolates, in a box lined with tissue paper and tied with a ribbon.

roasted pineapple marshmallows

The contrasting flavours of sharp pineapple and creamy marshmallows seem to go hand in hand and here the pineapple is roasted to really concentrate its flavour. These work well in a marshmallow salad – just omit the coconut topping.

1 ripe fresh pineapple, peeled, cored and cut into 5-cm/2-inch pieces

Basic Vanilla Marshmallows (see page 6 but follow method here)

2 tablespoons brown sugar

250 ml/1 cup cold pineapple juice

dessicated coconut, to decorate

Makes about 45 x 2.5-cm/1-inch cubed marshmallows

Preheat the grill/broiler to medium. To prepare the pineapple purée, arrange the pineapple pieces on a baking sheet and sprinkle with the brown sugar. Grill/broil for 10–15 minutes on one side before turning over. Grill/broil for an additional 5–10 minutes on the other side. Remove from the grill/broiler and let cool. When cool, transfer to a food processor and process to a purée. Refrigerate until cold. Measure out 250 ml/1 cup and set aside.

Prepare the marshmallows according to the recipe for Basic Vanilla Marshmallows on page 6, replacing the water with the pineapple juice in Steps 3 and 4, and adding the chilled pineapple purée with the vanilla extract with in Step 6.

Complete Step 7 and when the marshmallows are set, cut and top with dessicated coconut to serve.

sour cherry and cardamom marshmallows

A combination such as sour cherry and cardamom might sound intimidating, but the touch of the spice used in this recipe perfectly accentuates the beauty of the deep and delicious cherry flavour. These spiced treats are the perfect sweet bite for a cold winter's day.

Basic Vanilla Marshmallows (see page 6 but follow method here)

250 ml / 1 cup cold sour cherry juice

⅛ teaspoon ground cardamon

Makes about 45 x 2.5-cm / 1-inch cubed marshmallows

Prepare the marshmallows according to the recipe for Basic Vanilla Marshmallows on page 6, replacing the water with the sour cherry juice in Steps 3 and 4 and omitting the vanilla extract.

Complete Step 7 and when the marshmallows are set, cut into cubes and serve. These marshmallows have such a delicious flavour that they are best enjoyed just as they are.

hot chocolate

This recipe is for good, old-fashioned homemade hot chocolate – a marshmallow's best friend. By adding different flavoured marshmallows to the hot chocolate, you can create brand new hot chocolate flavour combinations, from candy bar chocolate heaven to rich raspberry chocolate – a delicious and warming treat for a cold day.

40 g/⅓ cup unsweetened cocoa powder

150 g/¾ cup granulated sugar

a pinch of fine salt

100 ml/⅓ cup of boiling water

950 ml/3¾ cups milk

60 ml/¼ cup single/light cream*

1 teaspoon vanilla extract

Makes 4 servings

Combine the cocoa powder, sugar and salt in a small saucepan set on the stovetop over low-medium heat. Slowly pour in the hot water and stir to combine. Simmer for about 2 minutes, stirring continuously and taking care not to burn.

Stir in the milk and cream and heat until the mixture is very hot, but not boiling. Remove from the heat and add the vanilla extract. Pour into cups and serve hot with your choice of marshmallow floating on the top.

*Or 870 ml/3½ cups milk and 120 ml/½ cup half and half

Some delicious hot chocolate and marshmallow combinations to try!

✿ For a **double chocolate delight** float a chocolate marshmallow (see page 14)

✿ For **candy bar chocolate heaven** add a chocolate-covered caramel swirl marshmallow (see page 22)

✿ For **peppermint chocolate bark** float a peppermint marshmallow (see page 16)

✿ For an **Irish cream dream** float an Irish cream marshmallow (see page 38)

✿ For a **rich raspberry chocolate** float a raspberry and rosewater marshmallow (see page 46)

✿ For a **soda fountain strawberry chocolate malted** float a strawberry malted marshmallow (see page 40)

treats

s'mores marshmallows

Traditional s'mores are scrumptious bites traditionally enjoyed around the camp fire. This version of the classic treat is a vanilla marshmallow topped with melted milk chocolate and sprinkled with crushed cookies.

Basic Vanilla Marshmallows (see page 6 but follow method here)

400 g/14 oz digestive biscuits or graham crackers

450 g/3 cups milk chocolate chips

Makes about 45 x 2.5-cm/1-inch cubed marshmallows.

Prepare the marshmallows according to the recipe for Basic Vanilla Marshmallows on page 6.

Put the digestive biscuits/graham crackers in a food processor and process to a medium–fine consistency. Set aside.

Prepare the melted chocolate according to the instructions on page 7. Working quickly, spoon 1–2 tablespoons of melted chocolate onto each marshmallow, letting the chocolate melt down the sides.

Sprinkle each chocolate-covered marshmallow with the crushed biscuits/crackers and set at room temperature or in the refrigerator.

Alternatively, to create a more traditional s'more, sandwich the chocolate-covered marshmallows between 2 biscuits/ crackers and toast over an open fire or heat in a warm oven for 1–2 minutes, just to melt the marshmallows.

gingerbread marshmallows

Gingerbread men are a traditional part of the festive season. Add a fun twist to this seasonal delight by making gingerbread marshmallow men and women. They are perfect accompaniments to hot chocolate or coffee. For an extra special holiday treat, they can be hung as ornaments on the Christmas tree. You can also make the vanilla snowmen on page 3 or any other shape you can find a cookie cutter for!

Basic Vanilla Marshmallows (see page 6 but follow method here)

1 teaspoon ground ginger

¾ teaspoon ground cinnamon

¼ teaspoon ground cloves

170 g/¼ cup black treacle/molasses (to replace the golden syrup/light corn syrup)

a gingerbread cutter, oiled

Makes about 22 gingerbread marshmallow men

Prepare the marshmallows according to the recipe for Basic Vanilla Marshmallows on page 6, adding the ginger, cinnamon and cloves to the water and gelatine in Step 3, replacing the golden syrup/light corn syrup with molasses and omitting the vanilla extract.

Complete Step 7 and when the marshmallows are set, use the gingerbread cutter to stamp out gingerbread men. If you want to use them an Christmas tree ornaments, use a cocktail stick to pierce a small hole in the top and thread through some narrow ribbon.

marshmallow fondue

1 quantity Chocolate
Marshmallows (see page 14)

1 quantity Raspberry and
Rosewater Marshmallows
(see page 46)

1 quantity Roasted Pineapple
Marshmallows (see page 49)

250 g/2 cups fresh strawberries,
hulled

3 ripe bananas, sliced

1 store-bought genoese
sponge/pound cake, cut into
bite-size pieces

225 g/8 oz double/heavy cream

350 g/12 oz dark chocolate

a pinch of fine salt

a fondue pot, or similar

Fondue comes from the French word 'fonder', which means 'to melt'. This indulgent sweet fondue recipe combines rich, melted chocolate with marshmallows in a variety of flavours, fresh strawberries, sliced bananas and cake to make the perfect dessert for sharing on a cold winter's night.

Prepare the three flavours of marshmallows according to the recipes on pages 14, 46 and 49.

Arrange the prepared marshmallows, strawberries, bananas and cake pieces on a plate.

Warm the cream in a heavy-based saucepan set on the stovetop over medium heat until it just starts to boil. Add the chocolate and salt and stir until fully incorporated.

Transfer the melted chocolate to the fondue pot, or similar, and set on low. Serve with the marshmallows, fruit and cake pieces with fondue forks for dipping.

chocolate marshmallow brownies

These irresistible brownies are best enjoyed while still warm if you want to fully experience the marshmallows melting into the gooey richness of the brownies.

112 g/½ cup butter

50 g/2 oz unsweetened dark chocolate (minimum 75% cocoa solids), broken into squares

200 g/1 cup granulated sugar

2 eggs

1 teaspoon vanilla extract

60 g/½ cup plain/all-purpose flour

¼ teaspoon fine salt

1 teaspoon baking powder

25 g/1 oz Basic Vanilla Marshmallows (see page 6), cut into 1-cm/½-inch pieces

a 20-cm/8-inch square brownie pan (or similar), greased and floured

Makes about 20 brownies

Preheat the oven to 175°C (350°F) Gas 4.

Melt the butter and the chocolate together in a heatproof bowl set over a saucepan of barely simmering water. (Make sure the base of the bowl does not touch the water.) Stir occasionally until smooth and combined. Remove from the heat and let cool slightly. Stir in the sugar, eggs and vanilla extract. Beat in the flour, salt and baking powder.

Spread half of the batter into the prepared brownie pan. Add three quarters of the marshmallows. Pour the other half of the brownie mixture over the chopped marshmallows and top with the rest of the marshmallows.

Bake in the preheated oven for 25–30 minutes, or until slightly springy in the middle. Leave to cool in the pan before removing and cutting into squares to serve.

the Elvis s'more

Peanut butter graham crackers

270 g/2¼ cups wholewheat flour

125 g/1 cup plain/all-purpose flour, plus extra for rolling

110 g/½ cup packed soft brown sugar

1 teaspoon baking powder

1 teaspoon fine salt

120 g/1 stick unsalted butter

60 g/¼ cup smooth peanut butter

170 g/½ cup maple syrup

125 ml/½ cup milk

2 teaspoons vanilla extract

Carmelized bananas

1 banana, sliced

1 teaspoon brown sugar

15 g/1 tablespoon unsalted butter

a pinch of fine salt

1 quantity Banana Peanut Butter Marshmallows (see page 14)

2 baking sheets lined with parchment paper

Makes about 48 graham crackers, or 24 s'mores

This indulgent s'more pays homage to the king of rock and roll, a man famous for his love of peanut butter, bananas and marshmallows – you'll be hooked after just one bite.

To make the peanut butter graham crackers, put the flour, sugar, baking powder and salt in a food processor. Pulse a few times to incorporate. Add the butter and peanut butter and blend the mixture to a coarse meal.

In a small bowl, whisk together the maple syrup, milk and vanilla extract. Add to the flour mixture and pulse a few times in the food processor until the mixture forms a soft and sticky dough. Lay out a large piece of clingfilm/plastic wrap and dust it lightly with flour, then turn the dough out onto it and shape it into a rectangle about 2.5 cm/1 inch thick. Wrap it, then chill in the refrigerator for about 2 hours or overnight, until firm.

Preheat the oven to 180°C (350°F) Gas 4.

When the dough is chilled, divide in half and return one half to the refrigerator. Sift an even layer of flour onto the work surface and roll the dough into a long rectangle about 5 mm/⅛ inch thick. Trim the edges of the rectangle to 10 cm/4 inches wide. Working with the shorter side of the rectangle parallel to the work surface, cut the dough into rectanglular crackers. Place the crackers on the prepared baking sheets. Chill for about 30–45 minutes in the refrigerator, until firm. Repeat with the other half of the chilled dough.

Mark a vertical line down the middle of each cracker, taking care not to cut through the dough. Using a toothpick, prick the dough to form two rows of dots on either side of the line. Bake the crackers in the preheated oven for 15–25 minutes, or until browned and slightly firm to the touch, rotating the sheets halfway through to ensure even baking.

To make the caramelized bananas, melt the butter in a small saucepan set over medium-high heat until it starts to brown. Add the sliced banana and sprinkle with brown sugar and a pinch of salt. Stir until the brown sugar melts and caramelizes the banana. Remove from the heat and set aside to cool.

To assemble, put a marshmallow on half of the graham crackers. Put a square of chocolate on top of each marshmallow and put two slices of caramelized banana on top. Finish each s'more with another graham cracker and roast the s'mores over an open fire or in the oven until the marshmallows and chocolate are melted. Serve immediately.

index